T0195617

HELP
IN TIME OF
NEED

FLOYD W. FLESHMAN

WESTBOW
PRESS®
A DIVISION OF THOMAS NELSON
& ZONDERVAN

All scripture quotations are taken from the Scofield Reference
Bible, the authorized King James Version, copyright 1909, 1917.
Copyright renewed 1937, 1945 by Oxford University Press, Inc.

This book is a work of non-fiction. Unless otherwise noted, the author
and the publisher make no explicit guarantees as to the accuracy of
the information contained in this book and in some cases, names
of people and places have been altered to protect their privacy.

WestBow Press books may be ordered through booksellers or by contacting:

WestBow Press
A Division of Thomas Nelson & Zondervan
1663 Liberty Drive
Bloomington, IN 47403
www.westbowpress.com
1 (866) 928-1240

Because of the dynamic nature of the Internet, any web addresses or
links contained in this book may have changed since publication and
may no longer be valid. The views expressed in this work are solely those
of the author and do not necessarily reflect the views of the publisher,
and the publisher hereby disclaims any responsibility for them.

Any people depicted in stock imagery provided by Getty Images are models,
and such images are being used for illustrative purposes only.
Certain stock imagery © Getty Images.

ISBN: 978-1-9736-2377-9 (sc)
ISBN: 978-1-9736-2376-2 (e)

Library of Congress Control Number: 2018903535

Print information available on the last page.

WestBow Press rev. date: 04/03/2018

This book is dedicated to my dad, Deacon Benny Fleshman, my mom, Beaulah Fleshman, and my brother, Deacon Kenneth Fleshman.

They Fought a Good Fight

Contents

Swimming

Lamentations 3:22 states, "It is of the Lord's mercies that we are not consumed, because his compassion fail not."

God's mercies keep us every day. As it is written, new mercies we see every day. If it had not been for the Lord being on our side, we would have perished a long time ago.

Testimony

When I was a young boy coming up in West Virginia, my dad didn't allow my brother Ernest and myself to go swimming. My brothers Bennie and Kenneth and Sister Delores were gone from home. My brother Bennie had gone to the city. My brother Kenneth had gone into the military and my sister Delores had gotten married and was living in the city. Ernest and I were the only children home with our parents at the time. I never could understand at that time why dad wouldn't allow Ernest and I to learn how to swim. During those times, you didn't ask your dad why, you just did what you were told.

Floyd W. Fleshman

This one summer, while hanging out with some of the older boys, I was thrown in the water and I had to learn how to swim anyway. As the years passed, I was told the reason why my dad didn't want my brother and I to learn how to swim. In that part of West Virginia where we lived, it was very mountainous. Therefore, there were a lot of coal mines in the area. Some of them were very large coal mines that the big companies owned and some of them were small coal mines called punch mines. Whenever all the coal had been taken out of the small punch mine, the company would leave and go to another area without doing anything about closing the mine or cleaning up the area. Whenever that happened, the dirt they had piled up on both sides of the front of the mine along with having to go up a hill in front of the two sides to get out, large ponds were formed because the water from the mine and the rain was not being pumped out. Some of the young people would go swimming in these ponds. My dad and some of his friends were swimming one day in one of those ponds and my dad decided to show his friends how good a diver he was. My dad made a swan dive and decided to keep his arms folded back at his side. He was not able to steer himself out of the dive when he entered the water, going straight to the bottom of the pond. There were some cable wires laying on the bottom of the pond that had been rolled up and left by the mining company. My dad landed straight up inside the cable wires and hit his head. With his arms folded back, it made it impossible for him to free himself. After a short period of time had passed, when he didn't come back up out the water, my dad's friends jumped in the water and saved him. Along with what happened to my dad, a boy who was a year older than me drowned in one of those ponds. This boy also dived in the water, went to the bottom and hit his head. The Lord had mercy on my dad and our entire family. If my dad had perished, my brothers, sister and I would not have been here. Thanks to the Lord forever.

Unsafe Job

Psalm 123:1 states, "He that keepeth thee will not slumber."

The Lord has proven Himself over and over and over again. He has not hidden the things He has done for us, but He has blessed us openly where all can see, over and over again. He has been our keeper and our provider. No one has kept us but the Lord. We are living in a world where all kinds of things happen to people and we are people who all kinds of things happen to. God keeps us through it all. Keep trusting in him.

Testimony

My dad worked in the coal mines of West Virginia. He was a hard worker and a safe worker even though he worked in an unsafe environment. A lot of men who worked during my dad's time died of black lung and other things because of the conditions and not having the proper protection when it came to equipment. Even though my dad had black lung, God blessed him to live to a ripe old age. Cars hauling coal ran on tracks in the mines where my dad worked. The cars were pulled by a motor that was operated by a man. To be able to get to and from the section of the mine you worked in, you had to ride in these cars. One day my dad finished his shift and got inside one of the cars to come out of the mine. The operator was running too fast when he went into a turn and overturned all the cars he was pulling. My dad was hurt badly. No one expected my dad to live. It was stated that every bone in his body was broken. The swelling was so profound that my dad looked as though he was going to explode. Everyone counted my dad out and no one counted the Lord in. I imagine that just about everyone, if not everyone, who counted my dad out at that time, died before my dad. My dad was two months, one week, and two days from his ninety second birthday when the Lord called him home. God is good.

Sickness

St. Mark 2:17 states, "They that are whole have no need of the physician, but they that are sick."

God has given us doctors when we are sick. It is God who has equipped the doctors with the things they need to be able to help us. It doesn't matter whether it is medicine, advice, surgery or anything else pertaining to our need, every good and perfect gift comes from the Lord. The doctors are our gifts from the Lord to help us. The knowledge of the sickness, what is needed to treat the sickness, understanding how to treat the sickness, the invention of the medicine and whatever else is involved, comes from the Lord. "A man can receive nothing, except it be given him from heaven" (St. John 3:27). Therefore, we should go to the doctor when we are sick. Thank God for doctors.

Testimony

When I was a little boy, on a hot, summer day, my mom passed out at home. There was no one there to help her.

During those times, living in the country where we lived in West Virginia, you could leave your house door open and not worry about anyone entering to cause you harm. So, as usual, mom had left the door open. We had this one neighbor, Mrs. Tucker, a friend of my mom's, walked over to our house and knocked on the door. After knocking and not getting an answer, she began to call out for my mom but still no answer. Mrs. Tucker, wondering if there could be something wrong, walked into the house and found my mom passed out on the floor. My mom was taken to the hospital and she was diagnosed as having very little blood in her body. I was told that the amount of blood was so small that the doctor said that he didn't know how she was living with such a small amount of blood. Later, it was discovered that she had a tumor that was causing the problem. I don't know how many pints of blood my mom was given, but I never forgot that event. I was so thankful for the blood that was given my mom that when I became an adult, I became a blood donor. If the Lord had not been on my mom's side by sending Mrs. Tucker by our house, my mom would not have survived. So, when we do get sick, let us not only just pray but let us also go to the doctor.

Hunger

St. Matthew 6:26 states, "Behold the fowls of the air: For they sow not, neither do they reap, nor gather into barns; yet your heavenly Father feedeth them. Are ye not much better than they?"

God is able to provide everything that we need. He is the source of everything that's needed. The Lord lets us know in St. Matthew 6:26 just how much He loves us and what we mean to Him. These promises should leave us without doubt in our minds as to what the Lord will do for us. He has told us and showed us that every promise is good, every promise is true and you can count on it. God's people don't have any reason to worry about going hungry and not being fed, God will provide. I am reminded of the widow woman at Zarephath who was gathering wood to cook the last of the meal in a barrel for her son and herself. The prophet Elijah went to her and asked her to make him a little cake first. The widow woman had said that she and her son would eat it and then die, because it was only a handful.

But after hearing the man of God, she did as he asked and made him a cake first. Because she obeyed the prophet, she did not run out of meal or oil. Just as the widow woman obeyed Elijah the prophet, we the people of God are blessed when we obey Him.

Testimony

Where I was raised up, coal was the number one industry. My dad was a coal miner and I remember when there were times when my dad was laid off because there wasn't any work. Sometimes the layoffs would last for quite some time. I remember how my dad had to get on a program for food so that we would have food to eat. I still remember the cheese, hash, powdered milk, powdered eggs, corn meal, flour and other food items. What I don't remember is ever going hungry or even missing a meal. My dad and mom faithfully served the Lord with gladness. My dad was a deacon for many years and he served in that office until his health would no longer allow him to serve. Because of my parents' faithfulness and the goodness of God and His promises to them, He never let us go hungry.

Minimum Wage

Philippians 4:19 states, "But my God shall supply your need according to his riches in glory by Christ Jesus."

The Bible tells us that we must work. Even in these times where most jobs pay very little money and the price for everything keeps going up. Wages are either going down or they can't keep up with the rising prices in this economy. Although we are in an economy where there are few good paying jobs, we must keep looking for that better paying job while working the current one. Sometimes a person must work a part time job along with the fulltime job to be able to make it. Sometimes we must leave to go out of state where there are jobs. God doesn't always bless you with a good paying job where you reside. If there are no good jobs available where you reside, you shouldn't expect God to make one available for you. Always ask the Lord what you should do. Put all your hope, trust and dependence in Him and He will come through for you.

Testimony

One year during one of those long layoffs from the coal mine, my dad left home and went to New York to work so he could take care of his family. There wasn't any work where we lived in West Virginia. A friend of my dad, who lived in New York, heard about my dad's situation, got my dad a job, and sent for him. My dad stayed there in New York until things got better in West Virginia. There is a song titled "He's an On-Time God" and that is what the Lord was to my dad, mom, brothers, sister and myself during those times. That is what the Lord is today to my family. He still is an on-time God, yes, He is.

Fishing

Psalm 118:1 states, "O give thanks unto the Lord, for He is good, because His mercy endureth forever."

I thank God for His mercy and His grace. If it wasn't for the goodness of the Lord, we wouldn't be here today. God has not forgotten us. He keeps watch over us every day. He's our helper and the only one we can depend on. Let us put all our trust in Him. He's always there for us in times of trouble and in times of need.

Testimony

I loved to fish when I was young. I went every chance I had. During the summer, after school had closed, my dad, younger brother, and I would go fishing quite often. One summer my dad let me go fishing with a family friend. The New River was about four miles from our home. We went fishing there most of the time. Mr. Woodson, our family friend, and I went fishing there that day. The New River was known for small mouth bass so that's what we were fishing for. Mr. Woodson passed me a gold spinner lure. He showed me another lure exactly like the one he had given me. He said to me, "You put this lure on your line and fish in front of me. I will follow behind you fishing and I will catch more fish than you." Most of the shoreline of the New River in our area was rocky so you had to be very careful where you stepped. You also had to watch for rattlesnakes. As we fished along the bank of the river, Mr. Woodson pointed to some green moss on some of the rocks and said to me, "See that green stuff there? Don't step in it. It's very slippery and you'll fall in the river." The New River didn't have a very good reputation in those days. My oldest brother, Bennie, once said that the New River had a devil in it because of the number of people who had drowned in it. As Mr. Woodson and I continued to walk the rocks fishing, I stepped in the green moss and went into the river. I didn't know how to swim at that time and I don't remember how I got to where I could walk out of the water. What I do know, and I'm very sure of is that the Lord has kept me all these years. There's no doubt in my mind about how I've arrived at this day. Through many dangers, toils, and snares I have already come. The Lord and Him alone has brought me this far. I am very thankful to Him for all that He has done for me and all my family.

The Law

Psalm 26:30 states, "He is our help and our shield."

The Lord is our help in time of trouble. There is no respecter of person by Him. He fights our battles for us. Who can fight against Him and win? If He is for you, He is more than the world against you.

Testimony

While in the military and stationed in Virginia in 1962, two friends and I walked over to Hampton Institute one summer day. As we were walking along one of the main streets in Hampton, I noticed a policeman walking his beat and coming toward us. The policeman, seeing who we were and walking abreast, moved from his side of the walkway on to the side where we were walking. I was the tallest of the three and was walking in the middle. I was nineteen years old at the time and never thought I would live to become grown anyway, so I said to my friends, "This is the day I die." The policeman and I walked into each other. It took him by surprise because I didn't move out of his way. He looked at me and didn't say one word. He backed up, went back to the side where he was walking, and went on. I told my friends that the policeman would never do that to anyone again. I could have easily been killed, but the Lord kept me. He is my help and my shield.

Falsely Accused

Psalm 108:12 states, "Give us help from trouble: for vain is the help of man."

God is always there to help us in time of need. He is our bridge over troubled waters. Even when we are falsely accused, He is there for us. Joseph was falsely accused by Potiphar's wife, but the Lord was his helper. And Joseph ended up being the governor over all of Egypt. We need to be like Joseph and keep the Lord first in our lives. When we do that, the Lord will always be there for us.

Testimony

I joined the Air Force after graduating from high school in 1961. After basic training, I went to technical school to become a jet mechanic. After finishing school, I was sent to Langley Air Force Base in Hampton, Virginia. While stationed there, I bought my first car, a 1953 Ford. It was a beautiful car and I took the best care of that car. One day while at work on the flight line, I was told to report to the First Sergeant's office on the double. So, I took off running to the First Sergeant's office thinking something had happened at home in West Virginia where my parents lived. When I got to the First Sergeant's office, there were two Air Force policemen waiting for me. They took me to their headquarters for questioning. I found out that someone had accused me of having their tires on my car. The person had taken the I.D. numbers off my car tires and turned them into the Air Force Police. The word got back to the flight line about what had happened to me. There was a Sergeant there who had worked the weekend. When he went to the cafeteria to eat, he noticed that there were two men under my car and wondered what they were doing. As soon as he heard what had happened to me, he reported what he had seen to the First Sergeant and I was cleared of the accusation. The Lord had placed someone who knew me and my car at work that weekend and sent him to the cafeteria the exact time that those men were under my car getting the I.D. numbers off my car tires. The Lord didn't allow anybody or anything to distract that Sergeant and keep him from seeing those men under my car. The Sergeant was on a mission from the Lord to save me and he didn't even know.

Reckless Driving

Romans 9:15 states, "I will have Mercy on whom I will have Mercy."

The Lord is plenteous in Mercy. New mercies are given each day. Whom so ever He chooses to have Mercy on is who He will have Mercy on. All of us have received mercy from the Lord. The Lord is a compassionate and Merciful God.

Testimony

After the birth of our first child in October 1965, my wife wanted to travel to Virginia the following summer and show her family our baby. She had planned to stay at least one month. When it was time to leave for Virginia, Charles, a friend of mine, wanted to ride along with us, since I was returning home after dropping off my wife and our baby. It was the summer of 1966 and my car was a 1965 Buick 225 convertible, just made for the road. From Cleveland, Ohio to Gloucester, Virginia was a pretty good drive, but we had an enjoyable trip going there. After spending Saturday and Saturday night in Gloucester,

Charles and I headed back on the long drive to Cleveland. Back then, Route 17 was a two-lane highway; one lane going North and one lane going South. As we were traveling North on Route 17, we were trailing behind a couple of cars that were not going too fast. Route 17 was country driving and had a few curves and a few small hills. Being cautious, some people drove slowly. After driving for some time, we finally came upon a stretch of road that we could pass on and there wasn't any oncoming traffic. I put my left signal on and went into the passing lane. Just as I was passing the car in front of me, the car came over and hit me. I tried to prevent the car from hitting me by jerking the steering wheel to the left, but the car hit me anyway. I went off the road and hit a line of trees as I was trying to keep control of the car. The driver side of my car was smashed in from hitting the trees. The man who was driving the other car stopped and the highway patrol was called. The state police arrived and placed both of us in the patrol car. I was placed in the back and the other man in the front. The state policeman asked the other man what had happened. The man began to tell the truth and suddenly started lying. I interrupted him and told him not to start lying. I preceded to tell the man a few things in the presence of the state policeman. The policeman saw how serious I was and immediately knew what was going on. The man in the front of the police car had thought the state policeman would take his side because of the color of my skin but his thinking was wrong. In the nineteen sixties, things were hard in Virginia for people of color. The Lord was watching over me and keeping me from harm and danger. The songwriter wrote, "Through many dangers, toils and snares I have already come. Tis grace hath brought me safe thus far, and grace will lead me home." So true.

Operation 1

Psalms 40:17 states, "Thou art my help and my deliverer."

Is there anything that God can't do? Are there things too hard for Him? No there is nothing that He can't do nor is there things too hard for Him. He is our help whenever trouble arises. He delivers us out of all trouble.

Testimony

My dad didn't talk very much. He was a man of few words, especially on the telephone. Whenever there was a call from home, it was always mom. One day, while living in Cleveland, Ohio, I received a telephone call from my dad. The call took place in 1968, three years after my wife and I had moved there. When I heard my dad's voice on the phone, I knew something was wrong. I asked my dad what was wrong and he told me that he was losing the feeling on the left side of his body. He needed back surgery and wanted to know what to do. During those times, back surgery was not good news because so many people came out of that type of surgery in bad shape. I reminded my dad that he was supposed to trust in the Lord and not in the doctor. I advised him to have the surgery. The surgery was a success. Because of my dad's back surgery, he couldn't work and there wasn't any income going into the house for my mom to live on and pay the bills. My dad had taken out an insurance policy in case anything happened to him, like surgery, and the insurance company would pay weekly payments until he could get back on his feet. The insurance company refused to pay, saying my dad needed surgery because of an old injury. At that time, I was working for an aluminum company outside of Cleveland. I had been working there for just a few years when my dad had back surgery. Everyone who had worked there for a minimum of one year was eligible for ten weeks of vacation time with thirteen weeks pay. I quit that job so that I could send money to my mom. During this time, my wife and I had one child. I had to get another job as quickly as possible. I got a job at one of the automotive companies outside of Cleveland. That job lasted around two and a half months. A few days after being laid off, I was sitting at a red light when one of the guys I had worked with, who was also laid off, called out my name from the other side of the light. He told me that another automotive company was hiring in the city. I went over and applied for a job and got the job. This was the company that I retired from in 1998. The Lord has truly been good beyond measure. Nobody or any other thing can work out something like that so perfectly. My family and I, including my mom, never missed out on anything. My dad was fine after the operation. Thanks to the Lord always for the great things He has done for me and my family.

Operation 2

Psalms 94:17 states, "Unless the Lord had been my help."

If the Lord doesn't help us, who can? So, we look to the hills where comes our help, because our help comes from the Lord. He is the only help that we know. He gives us grace and new mercies every day.

Testimony

In the late seventies, my dad was diagnosed with stomach cancer. On the day of the operation, my brother, Kenneth, my sister, Delores, and I were there along with my mom and brother, Ernest. Prior to the operation, the doctor came in and explained to us what could happen, even if the surgery was going correctly. For example, the doctor said that once a person's body was cut open, his organs could shut down. Even though that mattered to us, it really didn't matter because we knew that it was up to the good Lord as to what was going to happen to our dad. Having all our confidence and trust in the Lord and believing that everything was going to be alright, we formed a circle in the hallway and had prayer, making our request known unto God, who knew before we asked, what we were going to ask Him. During the operation, the doctor removed more than half of my dad's stomach. During my dad's recovery, he never had any pain so he never took any pain medicine. He fully recovered from the cancer and it never returned. The doctor had removed all the cancer during the surgery. Thanks to the Lord for His goodness to us.

Unbelief

St. Mark 9:24 states, "Help thou mine unbelief."

Every believer needed help with their unbelief to become a believer. Faith cometh by hearing and hearing by the word of God. God gives us all the help we need from His word. We are to believe all His word, not just some. We are to learn, love, and live His word. Jesus said if you love Him you will keep His commandments.

Testimony

My brothers, Kenneth and Ernest, and I would go with my dad to Appomattox, Virginia to hunt every Thanksgiving holiday. Appomattox is where my dad was born and a lot of rabbits could be found there. My dad loved hunting rabbits and squirrels. Uncle Richard, my dad's brother who lived in Detroit, Michigan, would meet us in Appomattox. We would always stay at the home place where Grandma lived prior to her death. Uncle Virgil, another of my dad's brothers lived in Appomattox with his family. We would all get together with family and friends and go hunting every Thanksgiving. During the Thanksgiving holiday of 1981, some of us were in the house talking about things that happened to us in the past. My dad and Uncle Richard started talking about spirits. As I sat there and listened. I couldn't believe that people could see spirits, although this wasn't the first time I had heard people could see them. I had heard my dad talk about seeing things. I knew my dad wouldn't lie but I still couldn't bring myself to believe that people could see spirits. The morning after the discussion about spirits, we headed out to the woods to hunt squirrels. As we entered the woods, we walked up a hill where the woods flattened out. We lined up there in a single line, apart from one another, but keeping one another in view as we walked. There were five of us in the line. To my right was my dad and to his right was Uncle Richard. To my left was my brother Ernest and to his left was my brother Kenneth. As we went forward hunting, there was a fence that separated my dad and I. While looking for squirrels on the ground and in the trees, I saw a squirrel nest in a tree that really caught my attention. I was thinking to myself just how beautiful that squirrel nest was. While I was looking up at the nest, everyone else kept walking. They had walked to where the woods went downhill and had gotten out of my sight. After thinking that I would never know whether a squirrel was in that nest, I started walking away. Just as I began walking, I heard a voice that was trying to get my attention. The voice sounded like the person was standing next to me. I stopped and said to myself, "I know I am here by myself." Then, I called out to my brother, Ernest, and he answered from far down in the woods. I needed comfort. I looked all around and no one was there, just like

I knew they weren't. I started walking off again and thought, "Turn and look again." So, I did. There was a man on the other side of the fence, walking away from me. The man was not there a moment ago. I could only see him from behind because he was walking away from me. For some reason that I can't explain, I thought he was my brother Kenneth. I said, "Kenneth, how did you get over there?" The man never said anything, but just kept on walking. I then turned and went to catch up with my dad. As I walked down the hill and caught up with my dad, he said to me, "Floyd, call your brothers and tell them to turn around. We're going back." I said to my dad, "I just saw Kenneth up on the hill behind you and Uncle Richard." Then I called my brother Ernest and told him to turn around because we were going back. Ernest then called Kenneth and told him the same thing. When I heard him call Kenneth, I was stunned. I then called Ernest and asked him if Kenneth was over there. He answered, "Yes." I then asked Ernest if Kenneth had been there a while. Once again, Ernest answered, "Yes." Immediately, I knew the Lord had shown me a spirit. There was no doubt in my mind what had happened to me. After Kenneth and I dropped our dad and brother Ernest off in West Virginia, we went to Cleveland, Ohio to our homes. It wasn't until I returned home that everything that had happened to me in the woods became reality. I cried and cried and was not able to stop myself from crying. I asked the Lord to let me live just a little while longer and I would get it right with His help. I immediately went out looking for a church for me and my family. From that day until this day, I never went back into the world that I was in. Since that day, it has been me and the Lord. The Lord helped my unbelief.

Job

St. Matthew 7:7 states, "Ask and it shall be given you."

God knows our every need. Even before you ask Him for a job, He knows you need one. After asking Him for a job, you then go out to find one and God will bless you with a job. Don't ask for a job and then refuse to go look for one. Jobs don't always come looking for you. If the Lord says, "Ask and it shall be given you," then it will surely come to pass if it is His will. God has made great promises to His children and they will all come into existence if you are His child. There are millions of people out of work and it doesn't look like it's going to get any better. God never said that He will take care of all your needs as long as times are good. He never said that if times get hard, He won't be able to help you.

Testimony

I worked for an automotive company in Cleveland, Ohio. In 1983, I was sent to a plant in Michigan, away from my family. In 1984, I was laid off from that plant and was told that the only place that was taking workers was in Louisiana. I asked the Lord to let me stay at home in Cleveland with my family and to not let me go any farther to work than Warren, Ohio. I was at home only a few days when I was told to report to work at the plant in Warren, Ohio. I had been told in Michigan that the only plant that was taking on workers was in Louisiana and I probably would go there. God knew what I would ask of Him before I asked. He had put everything in place for me before I even asked Him. I went to that plant in Warren, Ohio and stayed there until I retired in 1998. There is a song that has these words, "Trust and obey, there is no other way." There are no truer words that have been written by man to the children of God.

Wet Pavement

Psalm 27:9 states, "Thou hast been my help."

Man doesn't live by bread alone but by every word that comes from the mouth of God. It is God who keeps us.

Testimony

My youngest daughter, Felicia, left home in 1992 to go away to college to further her education. She attended Wright State University in Dayton, Ohio where her sister Tonya was attending already. Tonya had a male friend who owned a car. Tonya's friend let Felicia drive his car one rainy day. My daughter was driving too fast on the wet pavement and lost control of the car, wrecking it. I was told that she rolled the car. Another driver came along not too long after the accident and helped my daughter out of the car. The good Lord had it be that she only had a few bruises. God is plenteous in mercy.

Life Support

Psalm 46:1 states, "God is our refuge and strength, a very present help in trouble."

We have no reason to worry or be afraid under any circumstance. God is our refuge and strength. What is it that He can't do? God gives and God takes away. The Lord knows our needs better than we know ourselves. Just put all your trust in Him and He will bring you through whatever your situation may be. There's no failure in God. He specializes in things deemed impossible. He is able to do what no other power can do.

Testimony

When I lived in Cleveland, Ohio, I was a deacon at the church that my family and I belonged to. One of the deacons on the board became very ill and wasn't expected to live. People were saying that his chances to make it through were very slim. I hadn't been to visit him but was told how bad his situation appeared. One Sunday after morning worship service, one of the deacons invited me to go with him and some other members to visit deacon Williams at the hospital. I accepted the invitation and went with them to the hospital. The hospital was only about five minutes away. Five of us went to visit deacon Williams, four deacons and one member from the congregation. We went into the room to visit deacon Williams and I noticed that the member that was with us found it difficult to view what he saw. Deacon Williams was on life support with all types of lines hooked up to him. He was in a coma and his body was constantly jumping. I was asked by deacon Jamison to sing a song. I responded that I couldn't sing. Deacon Jamison said to me, "deacon Fleshman, you can sing. Sing deacon Williams' favorite song." The chairman of the Board of Deacons was with us. He was the best male singer in our church but deacon Jamison didn't ask him to sing. As I stood next to the bed, I began to sing "At the Cross." When I reached the part in the chorus with the lyrics, it was there by faith I received my sight," deacon Williams raised up in the bed with a smile on his face, his eyes still closed and then laid back down in the bed. Not long after our visit, deacon Williams recovered from his illness and returned to church. Some members of the hospital staff came to our church when deacon Williams returned. I guess they couldn't believe what had happened. Later, after deacon Williams returned to church, I asked him during Bible study one night if he remembered hearing me sing one day while I visited him. He said, "No." As time passed, deacon Williams' wife, two of the deacons and the member from the congregation who had visited with him that day in the hospital passed before deacon Williams. None of the people who went with me that day to visit deacon Williams in the hospital ever mentioned about deacon Williams raising up in the bed and smiling when I sang the song. I wondered about that. Did the Lord only let me see that? God is our life support.

Safety

Hebrews 4:16 states, "Let us therefore come boldly unto the throne of grace, that we may obtain mercy, and grace to help in time of need."

We are living in a time now when men are eviler than ever. The Bible states in II Timothy 3:13, "But evil men and seducers shall wax worse and worse, deceiving and being deceived." In St. Matthew 12: 43-45, Jesus tells of an unclean spirit who leaves out of a man but couldn't find any rest, so he returns to that same man and finds the place clean. So, he goes out and gets seven other spirits more wicked than himself and they enter in and dwell there and the last state of that man is worse than the first. We are now witnessing the truth of these scriptures. Men are going to the job killing people. They are going to our schools and our churches, killing children and adults. Terrorists are flying planes into buildings, setting off bombs in crowds of people, shooting people at airports, subways and places of entertainment, running people over with vehicles, stabbing and killing people in every way they can. We need the Lord's help now more than ever. The Lord said that He will be with us always even until the end of the world. He keeps His word, unlike man who is unable to keep his word all the time, although he may have meant what he said at the time. The Lord was with the Hebrew boys when the king had them put in the fiery furnace. The king had the fire about as hot as he could make it and it still wasn't hot enough to harm those boys because the Lord was their helper. The Lord was with Daniel when the king had him put in the lions' den. The Lord took all the wildness out of the lions and made them house cats. The Lord was Daniel's helper. We have a God that loves us and keeps us no matter how bad it gets. He supplies all our needs, even in times like these. Whenever we are faced with difficult times, we can always count on Him.

Testimony

Carolyn, a sister in the Lord and a friend of my wife and I, went to bed one night and left her son up watching television. The next morning, after leaving out of her room, Carolyn noticed that things were out of place. She observed that all the lights were on. The door to her son's bedroom was open so she looked in to find him asleep. She went downstairs and found all the lights on there. She looked and saw that the front door was open. Carolyn went to the bathroom and found the window open. She looked out the window and saw a bucket against the house that someone had used to climb in through the window. Whoever broke into her house had searched downstairs and upstairs. The person had also opened the door to her son's room. While all of these events were occurring, Carolyn nor her son had awakened. The Lord had caused Carolyn and her son to enter a deep sleep. When your house is invaded by a stranger, the situation is very dangerous. The Lord kept Carolyn and her son from being harmed by allowing them to sleep through the home invasion. God is always a very present help in trouble.

Red Light

Acts 26:22 states, "Having therefore obtained help of God."

There is no way we can make it out of serious situations without God's help. When things come upon us to take away our life, it is God who has the last say in the matter. God is the preserver of life.

Testimony

My wife and I have three daughters and no sons. As our daughters were growing up, it seemed like whatever the oldest daughter did, the other two daughters would follow. This was the case in most things. For example, our oldest daughter joined the school choir and so did our other two daughters. The oldest daughter went to college and the other two followed. The oldest daughter got married in 1995, the middle daughter got married in 1996, and the youngest daughter got married in 1997. All three daughters were pregnant together and had their babies close together in 1998. Our daughter Felicia had a boy, the first boy in our family. Not long after the baby was born, she had to take him back to the hospital to be examined. After leaving the hospital, she drove out to Cedar Avenue to the traffic light where Cedar Avenue goes uphill to Cleveland Heights. As my daughter proceeded through the light, which was green on her side, a car coming down Cedar Avenue failed to stop for the light and slammed into her. The man who hit my daughter was driving a sports car and she was driving a SUV. The sports car hit my daughter's SUV so hard that the front end of the sports car went down and under the SUV and the SUV ended up on top of the sports car. If Felicia had been driving a car or the man had been driving a larger car, the results could have been different. Neither my daughter nor my grandson were hurt. Thank God forever for His goodness.

Car Accident

Psalm 34:7 states, "The angel of the Lord encampeth round about them that fear him, and delivereth them."

Every child of God has an angel that is with him all the time. There is nothing that the angel can't deliver him from. The Lord gives his children an abundant life. His children have no reason to worry about anything.

Testimony

One summer my sister Delores and her family went out west on vacation. They were driving in the mountains on the west side of Denver, Colorado, going to Nevada. They were in two vehicles, following each other. My sister's husband, Francis, was driving the first vehicle and Delores was in the second vehicle with other family members. Francis stated that after he went around a curve, he looked in the rear-view mirror at the second vehicle and saw it come into the curve but it kept straight across the road. Francis also stated that he watched the car flip and start rolling over and over. Delores wasn't wearing a seat belt and was thrown out of the vehicle. She stayed in the hospital in Denver for about four months with a fractured pelvis from the accident. She made a full recovery. It has been said that serving the Lord will pay off after a while. I say serving the Lord pays off every day.

Beating

Psalm 118:13b states, "But the Lord helped me."

God is a God of grace, mercy, love, compassion and much more. His sun rises upon the unjust as well as the just. He feeds all mankind throughout the world. He does good to those that hate Him as well as those that love Him. There isn't a person living in this world that the Lord hasn't helped. "This poor man cried, and the Lord heard him, and saved him out of all his troubles" (Psalm 34:6). Help is what the Lord does. He's that kind of God. Put your trust in Him.

Testimony

I have a brother-in-law named Kevin who lives in Washington, D.C. Kevin is my wife's brother and he has been living in Washington, D. C. for quite some time now. In 2008, Kevin came very close to death. If it had not been for the Lord, Kevin would not be here today. Kevin and a friend of his shared an apartment. The apartment was located on the first floor. There was a tree right outside the window of the apartment. Someone stole a gun and hid it in the tree. Four young men went to Kevin's apartment looking for him, thinking he was the person who stole the gun. When asked about the gun, Kevin denied taking it. The four young men beat Kevin, almost to death. The emergency rescue team came and picked Kevin up and placed him in a body bag, thinking he was dead. A woman walked past the body bag and heard Kevin's moan which alerted the emergency rescue team that he was alive. Thanks to the good Lord and His help, Kevin is still alive today.

Doctor

Psalm 18:8 states, "It is better to trust in the Lord than to put confidence in man."

Man is human and is subject to error. God doesn't make mistakes. Man is born in sin and wrapped in iniquity. He sometimes has another agenda. When you have all your trust in the Lord, He will always work things out for your good.

Testimony

My brother Kenneth developed congestive heart failure and had to have a defibrillator inserted in his chest. As time passed, he began to have fluid buildup. Whenever this happened, he would have to go to the hospital to have the fluid removed and the doctors would check the defibrillator to be sure it was working correctly. One Thursday or Friday, Kenneth was experiencing shortness of breath and he called his son, Kenneth Jr., to take him to the hospital. Kenneth Jr. took his dad to the hospital and his dad was admitted to a room. After examining my brother, the doctor told Kenneth that his condition wasn't life threatening and he would get back to him on Monday. My cousin, Stanley was at the hospital on Monday visiting Kenneth when the nurse came in and informed my brother that the doctor would not get to him until Tuesday. My brother had been in the hospital four to five days with this condition. My cousin told me, when the nurse informed Kenneth that the doctor would see him on Tuesday, a very bad look of disappointment came across Kenneth's face.

Stanley was at the hospital on Tuesday when the nurse came in. She informed my brother Kenneth that the doctor had to see two other people before he came to see him. Stanley then asked the nurse if there was a problem since the doctor kept delaying seeing Kenneth. The nurse contacted the doctor and the doctor instructed her to bring Kenneth down. When my cousin Stanley informed me about the continued delays with Kenneth being seen and medically treated by the doctor, I was extremely upset because I was in Virginia and couldn't help my brother who was in Cleveland, Ohio.

I called my brother and asked him how he was doing. He responded that he was doing pretty well. The very next day, I called my brother and he told me that his breathing was becoming a problem again. I told him that I didn't think all of the fluid had been removed from his chest. I didn't rest well at all that night. I kept thinking that if I didn't get my brother from that hospital and doctor, he would not survive. The following day, I called my sister Delores who lived in Cleveland. I asked her to call my niece Mel, Kenneth's daughter, and instruct her to go to the hospital the next day and have the doctor assigned to Kenneth transfer him to Cleveland Clinic. I told my sister to inform Mel that I didn't want Kenneth to remain at that hospital another day and she was to remain at the hospital until the doctor transferred him.

When Mel arrived at the hospital the next day, she waited to talk to the doctor. The nurse came in and told her that my brother, Mel's dad, was going to be taken to hospice. Mel told the nurse that she was crazy for thinking her dad was going to hospice and demanded that her dad be transferred to Cleveland Clinic. Kenneth was transferred to Cleveland Clinic the next day. My brother lived several years after being released from Cleveland Clinic.

Love

I Thessalonians 4:9 states, "But as touching brotherly love ye need not that I write unto you: for ye yourselves are taught of God to love one another."

God never fails in anything. If God is teaching you to love, you will learn to love. What we must do is love the Lord, love His commandments, and obey. If we do these three things, then God will do what He said He would.

Testimony

My dad and mom served the Lord all their life. My dad was a deacon for many years until he became old and sick and could no longer serve in that office. The good Lord blessed my dad to live ninety-one years and my mom was blessed by the Lord to live ninety-six years. They never showed any difference when it came to people. They loved everyone even though everyone didn't love them. Everyone knew my parents and they were well respected by people. There was a time I thought they knew every preacher, deacon, and church member in the state of West Virginia. My dad never said too much about the problems he had with people over the years. My mom told me that she knew who loved her in the place of worship that she attended. Regardless of what was done or said to them, they continued to love those people. When the Lord teaches you to love, that is all you know to do. That's the kind of teacher He is.

Road Rage

Psalm 89:18 states, "For the Lord is our defense." Psalm 32:20 states, "He (the Lord) is our help and our shield."

The Lord is always there to defend and keep us in times of trouble. When our enemy comes to destroy us, the Lord will be our help. If the Lord is for us, He's more than the world against us. Don't fear what man can do.

Testimony

My wife and I have three adult daughters who have their own families. Our youngest daughter Felicia and her two children were living in Durham, North Carolina for a few years when Felicia decided to start looking for a better paying job. She found a job opening online in Norfolk, Virginia and decided to fill out the application for the job. She received a call for a job interview and drove to Norfolk. The interview went really well, and Felicia got the job. My wife and I drove to North Carolina and moved Felicia and her two children to Virginia to live with us while Felicia worked and looked for a place to live that was close to her new job. She had to drive over an hour to get to her job from where we lived. Both children had started school and were doing quite well. Felicia's son, who is her oldest child, was moved up a year at the high school because he had enough credits to just about graduate from high school. Felicia's daughter is five years younger than her brother and was a straight "A" student. Achieving all "A's" was an easy goal for her. After about two or three months, our daughter found a place that she liked that was closer to her job. Once again, my wife and I moved her and her daughter. Her son stayed with us because he only had a few months before high school graduation and we didn't want to interfere with his educational track.

Every Friday evening, we would meet Felicia approximately half the distance between our home and hers so that she could get her son to spend the weekends with her and his sister. One Friday evening, while traveling on interstate 64 to meet us at the usual place, our daughter and granddaughter were involved in a road rage incident. Felicia was driving in the right-hand lane when she noticed a car that was trying to merge onto the interstate. Felicia checked the left lane and observed a car in that lane which prevented her from moving over which would have allowed the car access that was trying to merge onto the interstate. The person attempting to merge onto the interstate was a college campus policeman who did not like it that Felicia didn't move into another lane. Although Felicia had the right of way, the man became enraged and followed her. Felicia noticed that when she changed lanes, the man changed lanes behind her. Felicia said she didn't think much of it at first, but noticed how close the car was driving behind her. When she realized that she was being followed, Felicia told her daughter to take a picture of the license plates on the car. A lady who was driving in the same direction noticed the situation occurring between Felicia's car and the man's car. When Felicia reached her exit ramp for route 17, the man who was following her exited behind her. The road was under construction and there was a large volume of traffic, due mainly to people traveling home from their jobs. As my daughter approached the slowed traffic in the construction zone, she applied her brakes. The man, who was following her so closely, drove into the back of her car. Felicia pulled over, stopped, looked in her rear-view mirror and saw the man getting out of his car, carrying a gun in his hand. The man walked up to her door and put the gun in her face. Felicia was really upset about the incident but was able to instruct her daughter to call 911. When the man saw Felicia's daughter use the phone, he went back to his car and remained there until the police arrived. The lady who had been driving in the same direction and observed the events that had unfolded, pulled over and waited with my daughter until the police arrived. The lady talked with the police and gave them her name and phone number, since she was a witness.

The police department, located in the area where the accident took place, investigated the case after my daughter requested that they do something about what happened to her. A complaint was filed against the campus policeman and he was taken to court. My daughter obtained a lawyer. The combination of my daughter's lawyer, the police department that filed my daughter's complaint, and the lady who was a witness proved to be a winning combination. The campus policeman received a consequence that was extremely fair for his crime. God fixed it. If it wasn't for the Lord, my daughter would have been dead. I am going to serve the Lord until I die.

Understanding

I Kings 3:9 states, "Give therefore thy servant an understanding heart to judge thy people."

God has everything we need. He is the source of understanding. If a Christian is lacking in understanding, ask God for it without doubting and He will give it to you. God wants us to come to Him for help. Wisdom is the principal thing and with all your getting, get understanding.

Testimony

When I worked for an automotive company in Michigan, I worked second shift, from 3 p.m. until you got off. You worked until what you thought was the end of your shift and an then announcement would be made over the intercom that told the time your shift would end. Regardless of the time I got off, I would always fix me something to eat when I got home. After eating, I would open my Bible and start studying God's word. Before I began to study, I would always ask the good Lord to bless me with knowledge and understanding. Sometimes, I would study until daybreak. I put all my trust in the good Lord because He said for man to have no confidence in man. I realized that God's word was the only word to believe because it was truth. I have asked the Lord for help in quite a few things on this Christian journey that I am on. He hasn't always given me the answer right away. A few years ago, I received things I asked for while in Michigan in 1983 and 1984. I had waited patiently for over 30 years for the answers. God answers all things in His own time. Whatever you ask of Him, whether it's wisdom, understanding, knowledge, or whatever it may be, be patient and wait on the Lord for it.

Other Books by the Author

The Rapture Deception

Printed in the United States
By Bookmasters